Look - Book 5
VI

By Viola & Zaida Stefano

The rights of Viola & Zaida Stefano to be identified as the authors of this work have been asserted by them in accordance with the **Copyright Amendment (Moral Rights) Act 2000.**

All rights reserved. Apart from any use as permitted by the authors & under the **Copyright Act 1968**, no part may be reproduced, copied, scanned, stored in a retrieval system, recorded, or shared, by any means or in any form, without prior written permission from the publisher.

A catalogue record of this book is available from the **National Library of Australia.**

ISBN: 978-0-6458482-2-9

Authors: Viola Stefano & Zaida Stefano
Illustrations, photographs, cover & internal designs: Zaida Stefano

Illustrations copyright © Zaida Stefano 2023
Design copyright © Zaida Stefano 2023

Disclaimer: The content presented in this book is meant for educational purposes only. The authors & publisher claim no accountability to any entity or person for any liability, damage, or loss caused or assumed to be caused directly or indirectly as a consequence of the application, use, or interpretation of the material in this book.

VeeZee Publications

Copyright © VeeZee Publications Pty Ltd 2023
First published in Australia in 2023
by VeeZee Publications Pty Ltd
veezeepublications.com

Learning made easy with

VeeZee!

- Focus Core words in 'Look - Book 5' and the 'Look' series (yellow)
- Secondary Core words in 'Look - Book 5' and the 'Look' series (blue)
- Other secondary Core words in the 'Look' series but **NOT** in 'Look - Book 5' (green)

Core Vocabulary used throughout **VeeZee Publications**				
I	**want**	**can**	stop	look
like	**more**	he	go	see
here	what	**do**	the	and
out	where	**we**	it	up
not	they	when	**that**	down
she	**now**	**them**	is	put
help	off	**you**	yes	on
turn	who	**this**	no	why
done	make	**a**	**to**	under
come	in	**some**	which	**there**
open	get	good	same	home

Supporting students with low vision (vision impairment - VI)

Our VI range has been especially developed to give children with low vision the very best opportunity to learn. The illustrations in the VI version of the readers, replicate key elements of the photographs included in the other version of the readers. We have done this so that all students engage with the same content. Yellow framing is used around each illustration to support children with low vision to focus on the illustrations more readily. Each book is carefully designed with deliberate and strategic use of colour, background and contrast for typescript and for illustrations. Placing these colours onto a black background supports children with low vision to see the illustrations more successfully because of the contrast provided. Teachers should provide guidance to their students by talking about the colours, lines and themes of each illustration. Ask questions using Core words; who, what, where, when and why, to reinforce their associations with surrounding words. The illustrations with their vibrant colours included in our VI range have been created to promote student interest, engagement and learning. Please ensure that classroom lighting provides optimal conditions for students to engage with the VI readers. We advise that students without a vision impairment also explore the readers designed for students with low vision. This will support interaction and discussion amongst the students. It is our hope that this will ultimately promote acceptance, understanding, compassion and teamwork, thus cultivating true inclusion.

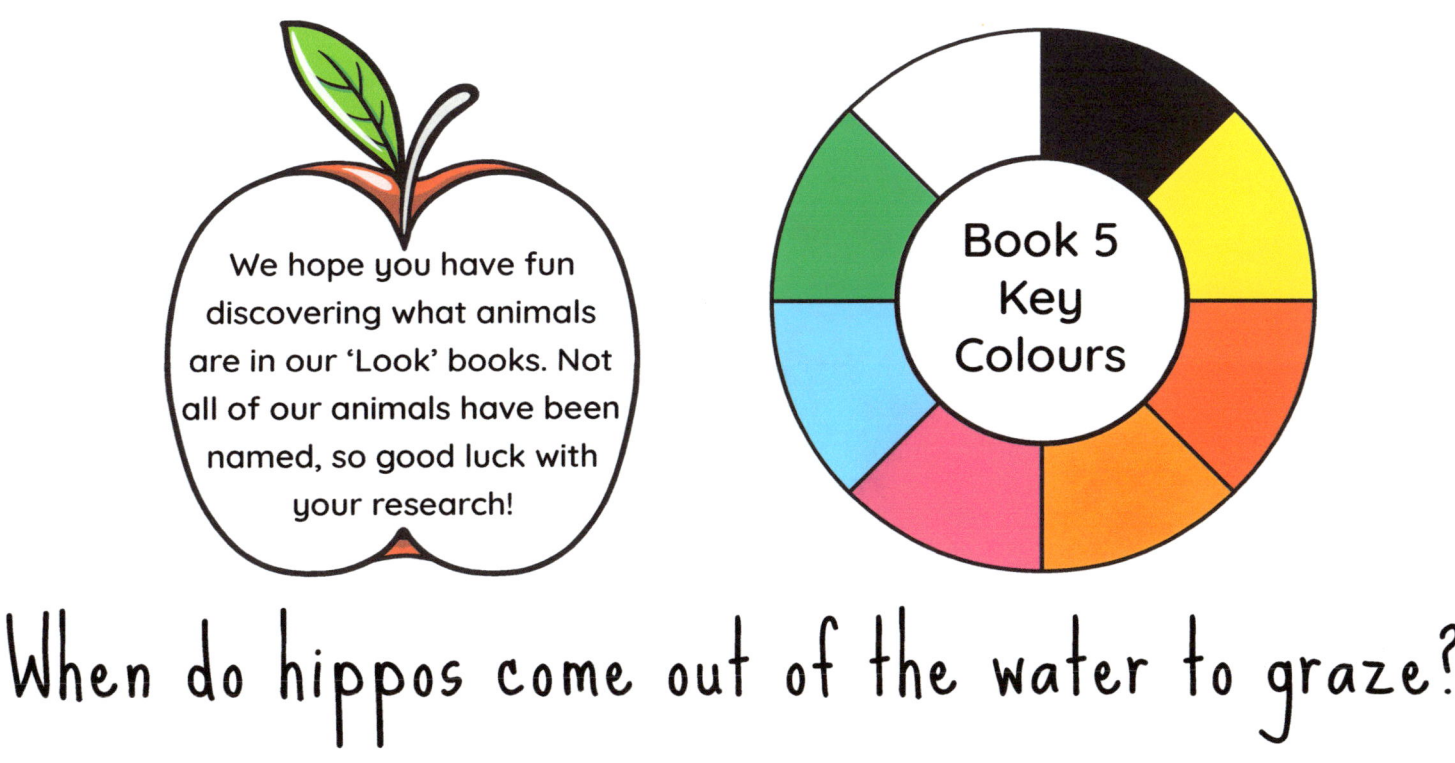

We hope you have fun discovering what animals are in our 'Look' books. Not all of our animals have been named, so good luck with your research!

Book 5 Key Colours

When do hippos come out of the water to graze?

Look. I can see a zebra.

Look. You can see a hippo.

Look. We can see that animal.

Look mum and dad. I want to see this.

I want to look here dad.

I want to look there mum.

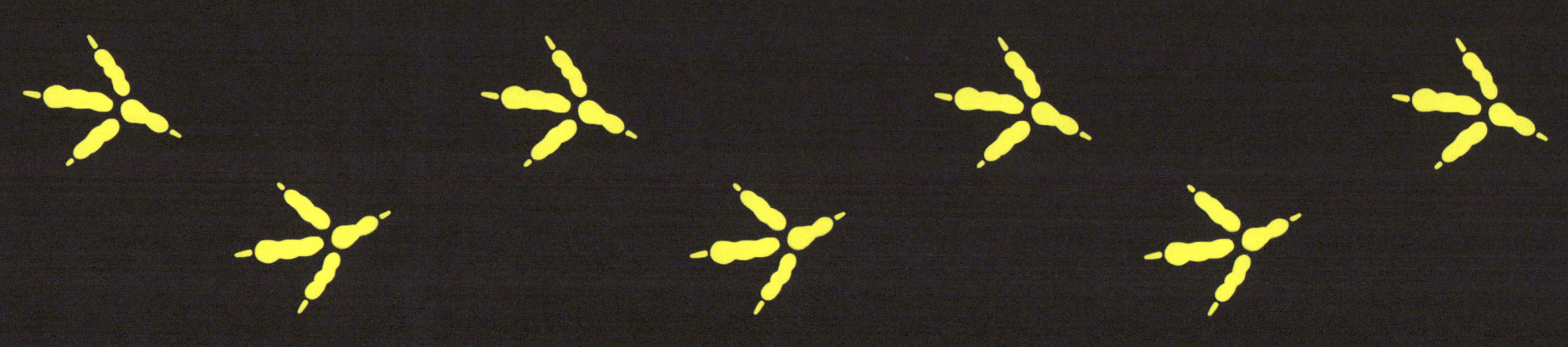

Look up there. I can see a bird.

Look down here. I can see the bird.

Come here now mum and look at this.

Look. Turn left and look at that.

Look. Turn right and look at them.

Look at this now mum and dad. It is a bird.

Look here now. No, not there. Look here!

Look at the zebra now. Yes, look here.

Look. I can see some more animals.

Look. We can look at it.

Look a lion! Do you like to look at it?

Words in this book

I	like	to
turn	down	up
here	look	there
can	mum	dad
come	hippo	some
right	want	a
zebra	animal	bird

Words in this book

at	it	left
this	the	not
that	and	see
you	more	we
now	them	is
lion	yes	no
animals	do	

Do you know the focus and secondary Core words: 'look', 'up' and 'down'? Read the words along each line.

look	up	look	down	look	look	down
down	look	up	look	up	look	up
look	down	look	down	up	look	up
down	look	up	down	look	up	look
down	look	look	look	up	look	up
look	look	up	look	down	look	look
look	look	up	look	look	up	down

Do you know the focus and secondary Core words in this book (refer to Core word table)? Find them along each line, point to them and say them. Read the other words too once you have pointed to the Core words.

I	the	look	it	we	like	animals
look	turn	like	mum	look	that	hippo
right	zebra	left	bird	dad	animal	look
some	up	look	is	that	them	see
a	this	want	there	more	can	at
and	to	no	you	yes	down	do
now	come	turn	look	not	here	lion

How many times did you read the word 'look'?

Make new words with 'we__', e.g., 'west'. Write sentences using these words.

Revision: 'Look' Books 1 – 5 - Read along each line.

Look. Do you like it?

Come look here mum and dad.

Look at them now, mum and dad.

Look at them here, and look at them there.

Turn right and look there now.

Turn left and look here now.

Look. Can you see it?

Look mum and dad. We can see them.

Look. I want to look down here.

Revision: 'Look' Books 1 – 5 - Read along each line.

I want to look there now.

I want to look at them now.

Mum and dad want to look at them too.

Turn back. Can you look here now?

Look. Turn right. We can look at it.

Look now. I can see more birds.

Look mum and dad. I want to see this.

We can turn left and look up at that.

Look here now. No, not there. Look here!

Revision: 'Look' Books 1 – 5 - Read along each line.

Look at the zebra now. Yes, look here.

Look down here. I can see some animals.

Look, that is a bird. We can look at it.

I	look	here	not	up	want
more	turn	we	you	this	the
see	to	like	and	them	there
now	come	a	some	can	no
do	is	that	down	it	yes

Fun activity - match the animals to the prints. Revisit the 'Look' books for clues.

43

Fun activity - match the animals to the prints. Revisit the 'Look' books for clues.

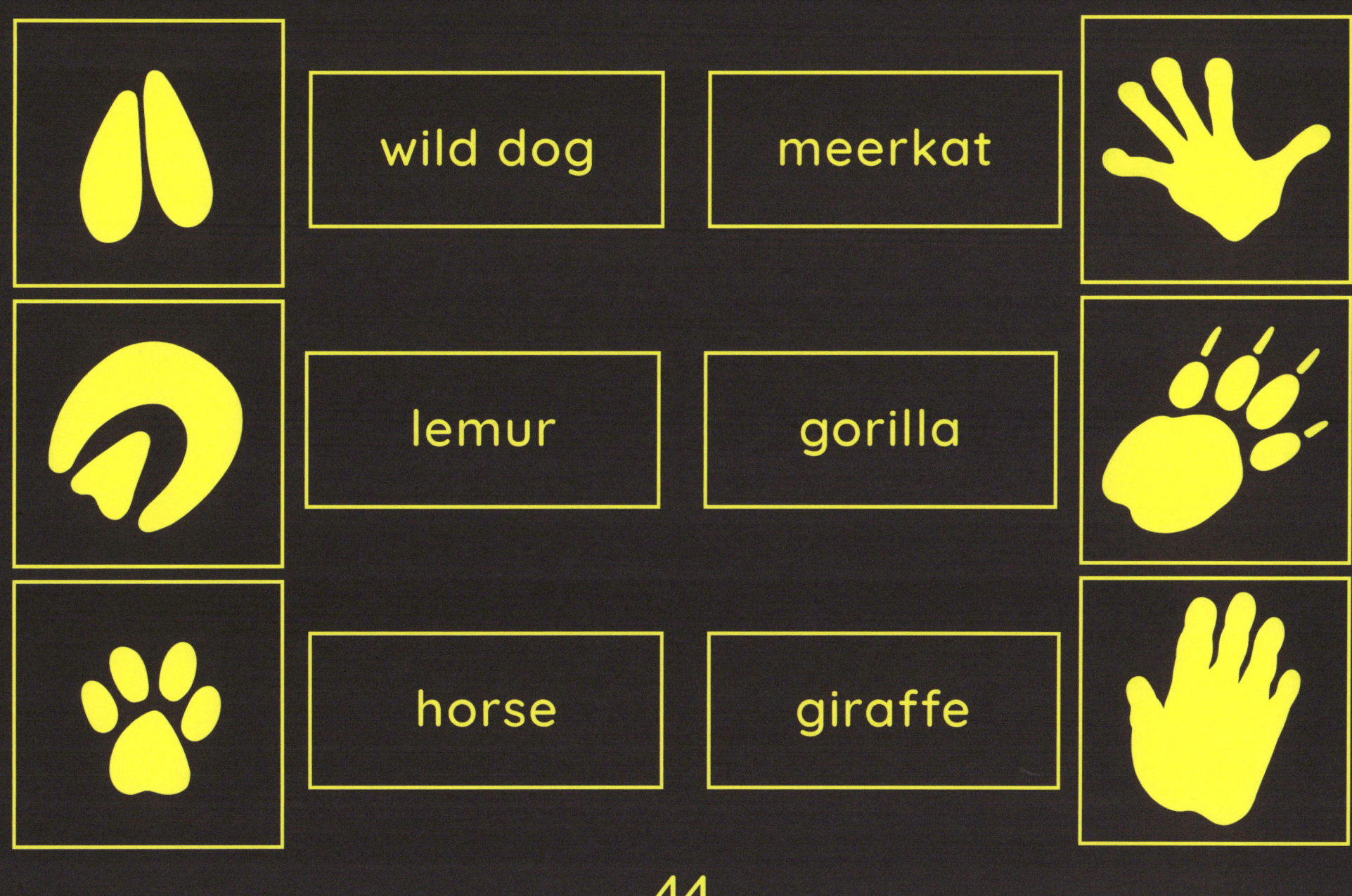

44

Fun activity - match the animals to the prints. Revisit the 'Look' books for clues.

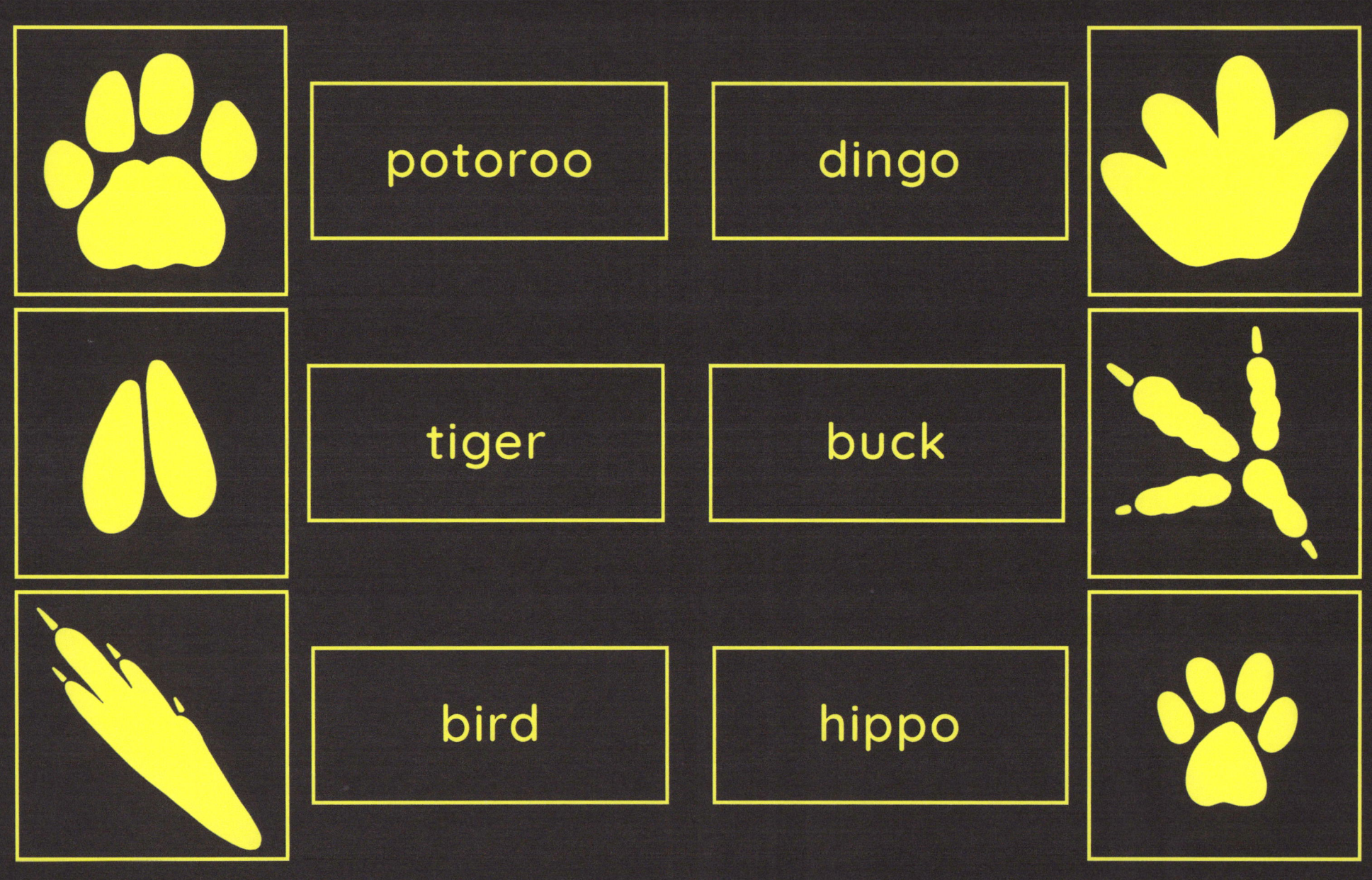

We hope you had fun reading!

VeeZee Publications

Wait, there's more!

Visit our website for information about our range of readers & supporting products.

veezeepublications.com

www.ingramcontent.com/pod-product-compliance
Lightning Source LLC
Chambersburg PA
CBHW050852010526
44107CB00047BA/1580